50 Healthy Food Recipes for Home

By: Kelly Johnson

Table of Contents

- Grilled Salmon with Lemon and Herbs
- Quinoa Salad with Roasted Vegetables
- Mediterranean Chickpea Salad
- Veggie Stir-Fry with Tofu
- Cauliflower Crust Pizza with Fresh Veggies
- Zucchini Noodles with Pesto and Cherry Tomatoes
- Black Bean and Corn Salad
- Stuffed Bell Peppers with Turkey and Quinoa
- Greek Yogurt Parfait with Fresh Berries
- Lentil Soup with Spinach and Tomatoes
- Avocado Toast with Poached Egg
- Baked Sweet Potato Fries
- Shrimp and Vegetable Skewers
- Tuna Salad Lettuce Wraps
- Roasted Brussels Sprouts with Balsamic Glaze
- Turkey and Veggie Meatballs
- Chicken and Vegetable Curry
- Greek Salad with Grilled Chicken
- Whole Wheat Pasta Primavera
- Quinoa Stuffed Bell Peppers
- Roasted Beet and Goat Cheese Salad
- Eggplant Parmesan with Marinara Sauce
- Spaghetti Squash with Tomato Basil Sauce
- Grilled Chicken Caesar Salad
- Roasted Asparagus with Lemon and Parmesan
- Teriyaki Salmon with Steamed Broccoli
- Lentil and Vegetable Stir-Fry
- Turkey and Black Bean Chili
- Caprese Salad with Fresh Mozzarella
- Baked Chicken Breast with Herbs
- Veggie and Bean Burrito Bowl
- Roasted Vegetable and Hummus Wrap
- Quinoa and Black Bean Stuffed Peppers
- Greek Yogurt Chicken Salad
- Veggie Omelette with Spinach and Mushrooms

- Turkey and Quinoa Stuffed Bell Peppers
- Baked Cod with Lemon and Garlic
- Cauliflower Fried Rice with Shrimp
- Chickpea and Vegetable Tagine
- Spinach and Feta Stuffed Chicken Breast
- Turkey and Sweet Potato Hash
- Grilled Vegetable and Hummus Sandwich
- Quinoa and Kale Salad with Lemon Dressing
- Broccoli and Cheese Stuffed Chicken Breast
- Greek Yogurt Pancakes with Fresh Berries
- Baked Chicken and Vegetable Casserole
- Lentil and Vegetable Soup
- Shrimp and Avocado Salad
- Baked Cod with Herbed Quinoa
- Chicken and Vegetable Skillet

Grilled Salmon with Lemon and Herbs

Ingredients:

- 4 salmon fillets (about 6 ounces each), skin-on or skinless
- 2 tablespoons olive oil
- 2 cloves garlic, minced
- 2 tablespoons fresh lemon juice
- Zest of 1 lemon
- 2 tablespoons chopped fresh herbs (such as dill, parsley, or thyme)
- Salt and pepper to taste
- Lemon slices for serving (optional)
- Fresh herbs for garnish (optional)

Instructions:

1. Preheat your grill to medium-high heat.
2. In a small bowl, whisk together the olive oil, minced garlic, lemon juice, lemon zest, and chopped fresh herbs.
3. Pat the salmon fillets dry with paper towels and season them with salt and pepper on both sides.
4. Brush the salmon fillets generously with the lemon and herb mixture, making sure to coat them evenly.
5. Place the salmon fillets on the preheated grill, skin-side down if using skin-on fillets. Close the grill lid and cook for about 4-5 minutes.
6. Carefully flip the salmon fillets using a spatula and continue grilling for another 4-5 minutes, or until the salmon is cooked through and flakes easily with a fork.
7. Remove the grilled salmon from the grill and transfer them to a serving plate.
8. Garnish with lemon slices and fresh herbs, if desired.
9. Serve the Grilled Salmon with Lemon and Herbs hot, accompanied by your favorite side dishes such as roasted vegetables, rice, or a fresh salad.

Enjoy the delicious flavor of grilled salmon infused with the bright and zesty flavors of lemon and fresh herbs!

Quinoa Salad with Roasted Vegetables

Ingredients:

For the Roasted Vegetables:

- 2 cups chopped vegetables (such as bell peppers, zucchini, eggplant, cherry tomatoes, red onion, or carrots)
- 2 tablespoons olive oil
- Salt and black pepper to taste
- 1 teaspoon dried herbs (such as thyme, rosemary, or oregano)

For the Quinoa Salad:

- 1 cup quinoa, rinsed
- 2 cups water or vegetable broth
- 1/4 cup chopped fresh parsley
- 1/4 cup chopped fresh cilantro
- 1/4 cup chopped fresh mint
- 1/4 cup chopped green onions
- 1/4 cup crumbled feta cheese (optional)
- 1/4 cup toasted pine nuts or chopped almonds (optional)

For the Lemon Dressing:

- 1/4 cup olive oil
- 2 tablespoons fresh lemon juice
- 1 teaspoon Dijon mustard
- 1 clove garlic, minced
- Salt and black pepper to taste

Instructions:

1. Preheat your oven to 400°F (200°C).
2. In a large mixing bowl, toss the chopped vegetables with olive oil, salt, black pepper, and dried herbs until evenly coated.

3. Spread the seasoned vegetables in a single layer on a baking sheet lined with parchment paper.
4. Roast the vegetables in the preheated oven for 20-25 minutes, or until they are tender and caramelized, stirring halfway through cooking.
5. While the vegetables are roasting, cook the quinoa. In a saucepan, combine the rinsed quinoa with water or vegetable broth. Bring to a boil, then reduce the heat to low, cover, and simmer for 15-20 minutes, or until the quinoa is cooked and the liquid is absorbed. Fluff the quinoa with a fork and let it cool slightly.
6. In a small bowl, whisk together the ingredients for the lemon dressing: olive oil, lemon juice, Dijon mustard, minced garlic, salt, and black pepper.
7. In a large mixing bowl, combine the cooked quinoa, roasted vegetables, chopped fresh parsley, chopped fresh cilantro, chopped fresh mint, chopped green onions, and crumbled feta cheese (if using).
8. Drizzle the lemon dressing over the quinoa salad and toss gently to coat everything evenly.
9. Taste and adjust the seasoning as needed, adding more salt, pepper, or lemon juice if desired.
10. Garnish the quinoa salad with toasted pine nuts or chopped almonds, if using.
11. Serve the Quinoa Salad with Roasted Vegetables at room temperature or chilled.

Enjoy this nutritious and delicious quinoa salad with the flavors of roasted vegetables and a zesty lemon dressing! It's perfect for meal prep and can be enjoyed as a main dish or a side dish for any occasion.

Mediterranean Chickpea Salad

Ingredients:

For the Salad:

- 2 cans (15 ounces each) chickpeas (garbanzo beans), drained and rinsed
- 1 English cucumber, diced
- 1 pint cherry tomatoes, halved
- 1/2 red onion, finely chopped
- 1/2 cup Kalamata olives, pitted and halved
- 1/4 cup chopped fresh parsley
- 1/4 cup chopped fresh mint
- 1/4 cup crumbled feta cheese (optional)
- Salt and black pepper to taste

For the Dressing:

- 1/4 cup extra virgin olive oil
- 2 tablespoons fresh lemon juice
- 1 clove garlic, minced
- 1 teaspoon dried oregano
- Salt and black pepper to taste

Instructions:

1. In a large mixing bowl, combine the drained and rinsed chickpeas, diced cucumber, halved cherry tomatoes, finely chopped red onion, halved Kalamata olives, chopped fresh parsley, and chopped fresh mint.
2. If using, add the crumbled feta cheese to the salad.
3. In a small bowl, whisk together the ingredients for the dressing: extra virgin olive oil, fresh lemon juice, minced garlic, dried oregano, salt, and black pepper.
4. Pour the dressing over the chickpea salad and toss gently to coat everything evenly.
5. Taste and adjust the seasoning as needed, adding more salt, pepper, or lemon juice if desired.

6. Let the Mediterranean Chickpea Salad sit for about 15-30 minutes to allow the flavors to meld together.
7. Serve the salad at room temperature or chilled.
8. Garnish with additional chopped fresh parsley or mint, if desired.

Enjoy this Mediterranean Chickpea Salad as a light and nutritious meal on its own, or serve it as a side dish with grilled chicken, fish, or lamb. It's perfect for picnics, potlucks, and summer gatherings!

Veggie Stir-Fry with Tofu

Ingredients:

For the Stir-Fry Sauce:

- 1/4 cup low-sodium soy sauce
- 2 tablespoons hoisin sauce
- 1 tablespoon rice vinegar
- 1 tablespoon honey or maple syrup
- 1 teaspoon sesame oil
- 2 cloves garlic, minced
- 1 teaspoon grated ginger
- 1 tablespoon cornstarch
- 1/4 cup water

For the Stir-Fry:

- 14 oz (400g) firm tofu, drained and pressed, cut into cubes
- 2 tablespoons vegetable oil
- 1 bell pepper, thinly sliced
- 1 carrot, julienned or thinly sliced
- 1 cup broccoli florets
- 1 cup sliced mushrooms
- 1 cup snow peas or sugar snap peas
- 2 green onions, sliced
- Cooked rice or noodles, for serving
- Sesame seeds and sliced green onions for garnish (optional)

Instructions:

1. In a small bowl, whisk together the ingredients for the stir-fry sauce: soy sauce, hoisin sauce, rice vinegar, honey or maple syrup, sesame oil, minced garlic, grated ginger, cornstarch, and water. Set aside.
2. Heat 1 tablespoon of vegetable oil in a large skillet or wok over medium-high heat. Add the cubed tofu and cook until golden brown on all sides, about 5-7 minutes. Remove the tofu from the skillet and set aside.
3. In the same skillet, add the remaining 1 tablespoon of vegetable oil. Add the sliced bell pepper, julienned carrot, broccoli florets, sliced mushrooms, and snow

      peas or sugar snap peas. Stir-fry for 3-4 minutes, or until the vegetables are tender-crisp.
4. Return the cooked tofu to the skillet with the vegetables.
5. Pour the stir-fry sauce over the tofu and vegetables in the skillet. Stir well to coat everything evenly.
6. Cook for an additional 2-3 minutes, or until the sauce has thickened and the tofu and vegetables are heated through.
7. Remove from heat and stir in the sliced green onions.
8. Serve the Veggie Stir-Fry with Tofu hot over cooked rice or noodles.
9. Garnish with sesame seeds and additional sliced green onions, if desired.

Enjoy this delicious and nutritious Veggie Stir-Fry with Tofu as a satisfying vegetarian meal! Feel free to customize the vegetables according to your preference or what you have on hand.

Cauliflower Crust Pizza with Fresh Veggies

Ingredients:

For the Cauliflower Crust:

- 1 medium head cauliflower, cut into florets
- 1/2 cup shredded mozzarella cheese
- 1/4 cup grated Parmesan cheese
- 1/2 teaspoon dried oregano
- 1/2 teaspoon dried basil
- 1/4 teaspoon garlic powder
- 1/4 teaspoon onion powder
- Salt and black pepper to taste
- 1 egg, beaten

For the Toppings:

- 1/2 cup pizza sauce or marinara sauce
- 1 cup shredded mozzarella cheese
- Assorted fresh veggies (such as sliced bell peppers, cherry tomatoes, sliced mushrooms, sliced red onion, baby spinach leaves, etc.)
- Fresh basil leaves for garnish (optional)

Instructions:

1. Preheat your oven to 425°F (220°C). Line a baking sheet or pizza pan with parchment paper.
2. Place the cauliflower florets in a food processor and pulse until they resemble fine crumbs, similar to rice.
3. Transfer the cauliflower crumbs to a microwave-safe bowl and microwave on high for 4-5 minutes, or until softened.
4. Allow the cooked cauliflower to cool slightly, then transfer it to a clean kitchen towel or cheesecloth. Squeeze out as much excess moisture as possible.
5. In a large mixing bowl, combine the squeezed cauliflower, shredded mozzarella cheese, grated Parmesan cheese, dried oregano, dried basil, garlic powder, onion powder, salt, black pepper, and beaten egg. Mix until well combined.

6. Transfer the cauliflower mixture to the prepared baking sheet or pizza pan. Use your hands to press the mixture into a thin, even crust shape, about 1/4 inch thick.
7. Bake the cauliflower crust in the preheated oven for 15-20 minutes, or until golden brown and crisp around the edges.
8. Remove the cauliflower crust from the oven and spread the pizza sauce or marinara sauce evenly over the crust.
9. Sprinkle the shredded mozzarella cheese over the sauce.
10. Arrange the assorted fresh veggies on top of the cheese.
11. Return the pizza to the oven and bake for an additional 10-15 minutes, or until the cheese is melted and bubbly, and the crust is golden brown.
12. Remove the cauliflower crust pizza from the oven and let it cool slightly before slicing.
13. Garnish with fresh basil leaves, if desired.
14. Slice the Cauliflower Crust Pizza with Fresh Veggies and serve hot.

Enjoy this delicious and nutritious Cauliflower Crust Pizza with your favorite fresh veggies for a satisfying meal!

Zucchini Noodles with Pesto and Cherry Tomatoes

Ingredients:

For the Pesto:

- 2 cups fresh basil leaves, packed
- 1/3 cup grated Parmesan cheese
- 1/4 cup pine nuts or walnuts
- 2 cloves garlic, minced
- 1/3 cup extra virgin olive oil
- Salt and black pepper to taste

For the Zucchini Noodles:

- 4 medium zucchini, spiralized or julienned into noodles
- 1 tablespoon olive oil
- 1 pint cherry tomatoes, halved
- Salt and black pepper to taste
- Grated Parmesan cheese for serving (optional)
- Fresh basil leaves for garnish (optional)

Instructions:

1. To make the pesto, combine the fresh basil leaves, grated Parmesan cheese, pine nuts or walnuts, and minced garlic in a food processor. Pulse until coarsely chopped.
2. With the food processor running, slowly drizzle in the olive oil until the pesto is smooth and well combined. Season with salt and black pepper to taste. Set aside.
3. Heat the olive oil in a large skillet over medium heat. Add the cherry tomatoes to the skillet and cook for 3-4 minutes, or until they start to soften and release their juices.
4. Add the zucchini noodles to the skillet with the cherry tomatoes. Cook for 2-3 minutes, tossing gently, until the zucchini noodles are just tender but still crisp.
5. Remove the skillet from heat and stir in the pesto until the zucchini noodles are evenly coated.

6. Taste and adjust the seasoning with salt and black pepper if needed.
7. Serve the Zucchini Noodles with Pesto and Cherry Tomatoes hot, garnished with grated Parmesan cheese and fresh basil leaves if desired.

Enjoy this light and flavorful dish as a satisfying and nutritious meal! It's perfect for a quick weeknight dinner or a light lunch.

Black Bean and Corn Salad

Ingredients:

- 2 cans (15 ounces each) black beans, drained and rinsed
- 2 cups frozen corn kernels, thawed
- 1 red bell pepper, diced
- 1/2 red onion, finely chopped
- 1/4 cup chopped fresh cilantro
- 1 jalapeño pepper, seeded and finely chopped (optional)
- 2 tablespoons extra virgin olive oil
- 2 tablespoons fresh lime juice
- 1 teaspoon ground cumin
- 1/2 teaspoon chili powder
- Salt and black pepper to taste
- Avocado slices for garnish (optional)
- Lime wedges for serving (optional)

Instructions:

1. In a large mixing bowl, combine the black beans, corn kernels, diced red bell pepper, finely chopped red onion, chopped fresh cilantro, and finely chopped jalapeño pepper (if using).
2. In a small bowl, whisk together the extra virgin olive oil, fresh lime juice, ground cumin, chili powder, salt, and black pepper to make the dressing.
3. Pour the dressing over the black bean and corn mixture in the large bowl. Toss gently to coat everything evenly.
4. Taste and adjust the seasoning with more salt, black pepper, or lime juice if needed.
5. Cover the bowl and refrigerate the Black Bean and Corn Salad for at least 30 minutes to allow the flavors to meld together.
6. Before serving, give the salad a quick stir and garnish with avocado slices and lime wedges if desired.
7. Serve the Black Bean and Corn Salad chilled or at room temperature.

Enjoy this delicious and colorful Black Bean and Corn Salad as a healthy and satisfying side dish or as a light meal on its own! It's packed with fiber, protein, and flavor, making it a crowd-pleaser for any occasion.

Stuffed Bell Peppers with Turkey and Quinoa

Ingredients:

- 4 large bell peppers, any color
- 1 cup quinoa, rinsed
- 2 cups water or vegetable broth
- 1 tablespoon olive oil
- 1 small onion, finely chopped
- 2 cloves garlic, minced
- 1 pound ground turkey
- 1 teaspoon ground cumin
- 1 teaspoon paprika
- 1/2 teaspoon dried oregano
- Salt and black pepper to taste
- 1 (15-ounce) can black beans, drained and rinsed
- 1 cup corn kernels (fresh, frozen, or canned)
- 1 cup diced tomatoes (fresh or canned)
- 1/2 cup shredded cheddar or Monterey Jack cheese (optional)
- Chopped fresh cilantro or parsley for garnish (optional)

Instructions:

1. Preheat your oven to 375°F (190°C). Grease a baking dish large enough to hold the bell peppers.
2. Cut the tops off the bell peppers and remove the seeds and membranes. If the bell peppers don't stand upright, slice a thin layer from the bottom to create a flat surface.
3. In a saucepan, combine the rinsed quinoa and water or vegetable broth. Bring to a boil, then reduce the heat to low, cover, and simmer for 15-20 minutes, or until the quinoa is cooked and the liquid is absorbed.
4. In a large skillet, heat the olive oil over medium heat. Add the chopped onion and minced garlic, and cook until softened, about 3-4 minutes.
5. Add the ground turkey to the skillet, breaking it up with a spoon. Cook until the turkey is browned and cooked through, about 5-6 minutes.
6. Stir in the ground cumin, paprika, dried oregano, salt, and black pepper. Cook for an additional 2-3 minutes to toast the spices.

7. Add the cooked quinoa, black beans, corn kernels, and diced tomatoes to the skillet with the turkey mixture. Stir well to combine and cook for another 2-3 minutes to heat everything through.
8. Taste and adjust the seasoning if needed.
9. Stuff the bell peppers with the turkey and quinoa mixture, pressing down gently to pack the filling.
10. Place the stuffed bell peppers upright in the prepared baking dish. If there's any leftover filling, you can spoon it around the peppers in the dish.
11. If using cheese, sprinkle the shredded cheddar or Monterey Jack cheese over the tops of the stuffed bell peppers.
12. Cover the baking dish with aluminum foil and bake in the preheated oven for 25-30 minutes, or until the bell peppers are tender.
13. Remove the foil and bake for an additional 5 minutes, or until the cheese is melted and bubbly.
14. Remove the stuffed bell peppers from the oven and let them cool for a few minutes before serving.
15. Garnish with chopped fresh cilantro or parsley if desired.

Enjoy these delicious Stuffed Bell Peppers with Turkey and Quinoa as a wholesome and satisfying meal! They're perfect for a family dinner or meal prep for the week ahead.

Greek Yogurt Parfait with Fresh Berries

Ingredients:

- 1 cup Greek yogurt (plain or flavored)
- 1/2 cup fresh berries (such as strawberries, blueberries, raspberries, or blackberries)
- 1/4 cup granola
- 1 tablespoon honey or maple syrup (optional)
- Fresh mint leaves for garnish (optional)

Instructions:

1. If using plain Greek yogurt, you can sweeten it by stirring in honey or maple syrup to taste.
2. In a glass or bowl, layer the Greek yogurt with fresh berries and granola.
3. Start with a spoonful of Greek yogurt at the bottom of the glass, followed by a layer of fresh berries, and then a layer of granola. Repeat until the glass is filled, ending with a layer of granola on top.
4. Garnish with fresh mint leaves for a pop of color and flavor, if desired.
5. Serve the Greek Yogurt Parfait immediately and enjoy!

Feel free to customize your parfait by adding other toppings such as nuts, seeds, coconut flakes, or a drizzle of nut butter. You can also experiment with different flavors of Greek yogurt or mix in some vanilla extract for added sweetness. This versatile recipe is perfect for a quick and healthy breakfast on busy mornings or as a satisfying snack any time of day.

Lentil Soup with Spinach and Tomatoes

Ingredients:

- 1 cup dried green or brown lentils, rinsed and drained
- 1 tablespoon olive oil
- 1 onion, finely chopped
- 2 cloves garlic, minced
- 2 carrots, diced
- 2 celery stalks, diced
- 1 teaspoon ground cumin
- 1 teaspoon ground coriander
- 1/2 teaspoon smoked paprika
- 1/4 teaspoon red pepper flakes (optional, for heat)
- 1 (14.5-ounce) can diced tomatoes
- 4 cups vegetable broth or water
- 2 cups fresh spinach leaves, chopped
- Salt and black pepper to taste
- Fresh lemon juice, for serving (optional)
- Chopped fresh parsley or cilantro for garnish (optional)

Instructions:

1. In a large pot or Dutch oven, heat the olive oil over medium heat. Add the chopped onion and cook until softened, about 5 minutes.
2. Add the minced garlic, diced carrots, and diced celery to the pot. Cook for another 3-4 minutes, stirring occasionally.
3. Stir in the ground cumin, ground coriander, smoked paprika, and red pepper flakes (if using). Cook for 1-2 minutes to toast the spices and release their flavors.
4. Add the rinsed and drained lentils to the pot, along with the diced tomatoes (including their juices) and vegetable broth or water.
5. Bring the soup to a boil, then reduce the heat to low and simmer, covered, for 20-25 minutes, or until the lentils are tender.
6. Stir in the chopped fresh spinach leaves and cook for an additional 2-3 minutes, or until the spinach is wilted.

7. Season the Lentil Soup with Spinach and Tomatoes with salt and black pepper to taste. If the soup is too thick, you can add more vegetable broth or water to reach your desired consistency.
8. Remove the soup from heat and squeeze in some fresh lemon juice to brighten the flavors, if desired.
9. Ladle the soup into bowls and garnish with chopped fresh parsley or cilantro, if using.
10. Serve the Lentil Soup with Spinach and Tomatoes hot, accompanied by crusty bread or your favorite side dish.

Enjoy this delicious and nutritious Lentil Soup with Spinach and Tomatoes for a comforting and satisfying meal! It's packed with protein, fiber, and plenty of flavor.

Avocado Toast with Poached Egg

Ingredients:

- 2 slices of whole grain bread
- 1 ripe avocado
- 2 eggs
- 1 teaspoon white vinegar (for poaching eggs)
- Salt and black pepper to taste
- Red pepper flakes (optional, for garnish)
- Fresh herbs such as chopped cilantro, parsley, or chives (optional, for garnish)

Instructions:

1. Toast the slices of whole grain bread until golden brown and crispy.
2. While the bread is toasting, prepare the avocado. Cut the avocado in half lengthwise and remove the pit. Scoop the flesh into a bowl and mash it with a fork until smooth. Season with salt and black pepper to taste.
3. In a large skillet or saucepan, bring water to a gentle simmer. Add the white vinegar, which helps the eggs keep their shape while poaching.
4. Crack each egg into a small bowl or ramekin. Gently slide the eggs, one at a time, into the simmering water. Poach the eggs for about 3-4 minutes, or until the whites are set but the yolks are still runny.
5. While the eggs are poaching, spread the mashed avocado evenly onto the toasted bread slices.
6. Using a slotted spoon, carefully remove the poached eggs from the water and drain off any excess water. Place one poached egg on top of each slice of avocado toast.
7. Season the poached eggs with a sprinkle of salt, black pepper, and red pepper flakes, if desired.
8. Garnish the Avocado Toast with Poached Egg with fresh herbs such as chopped cilantro, parsley, or chives, for added flavor and color.
9. Serve the Avocado Toast with Poached Egg immediately, while the eggs are still warm and the yolks are runny.

Enjoy this delicious and nutritious Avocado Toast with Poached Egg for a satisfying and wholesome breakfast or brunch! It's a simple yet elegant dish that's sure to become a favorite.

Baked Sweet Potato Fries

Ingredients:

- 2 medium sweet potatoes, peeled
- 2 tablespoons olive oil
- 1 teaspoon paprika
- 1/2 teaspoon garlic powder
- 1/2 teaspoon onion powder
- 1/2 teaspoon cumin
- Salt and black pepper to taste
- Fresh parsley or cilantro for garnish (optional)

Instructions:

1. Preheat your oven to 425°F (220°C) and line a baking sheet with parchment paper or aluminum foil.
2. Cut the peeled sweet potatoes into evenly sized fries, about 1/4 to 1/2 inch thick.
3. In a large bowl, toss the sweet potato fries with olive oil, paprika, garlic powder, onion powder, cumin, salt, and black pepper until evenly coated.
4. Arrange the seasoned sweet potato fries in a single layer on the prepared baking sheet, making sure they are not crowded to ensure even cooking and crispiness.
5. Bake in the preheated oven for 20-25 minutes, flipping the fries halfway through, until they are golden brown and crispy on the outside and tender on the inside.
6. Remove the baked sweet potato fries from the oven and let them cool slightly before serving.
7. Garnish with fresh parsley or cilantro, if desired, and serve hot.

These Baked Sweet Potato Fries are delicious on their own or served with your favorite dipping sauce, such as ketchup, aioli, or sriracha mayo. Enjoy them as a healthier snack or side dish for any meal!

Shrimp and Vegetable Skewers

Ingredients:

- 1 pound large shrimp, peeled and deveined
- 2 bell peppers (any color), cut into chunks
- 1 red onion, cut into chunks
- 1 zucchini, sliced
- 8-10 cherry tomatoes
- Wooden skewers, soaked in water for 30 minutes to prevent burning

For the marinade:

- 1/4 cup olive oil
- 2 cloves garlic, minced
- 1 tablespoon lemon juice
- 1 teaspoon paprika
- 1 teaspoon dried oregano
- Salt and pepper to taste

Instructions:

1. In a bowl, whisk together the olive oil, minced garlic, lemon juice, paprika, dried oregano, salt, and pepper to make the marinade.
2. Place the shrimp in a separate bowl and pour half of the marinade over them. Toss to coat the shrimp evenly. Reserve the other half of the marinade for the vegetables.
3. Thread the marinated shrimp onto the soaked wooden skewers, alternating with the bell peppers, red onion, zucchini, and cherry tomatoes.
4. Brush the vegetable skewers with the remaining marinade.
5. Preheat your grill or grill pan over medium-high heat. If you're using an outdoor grill, make sure it's lightly oiled to prevent sticking.
6. Place the skewers on the grill and cook for about 2-3 minutes per side, or until the shrimp are pink and opaque and the vegetables are tender and lightly charred.
7. Remove the skewers from the grill and serve immediately, garnished with chopped fresh parsley or cilantro, if desired.

These shrimp and vegetable skewers are perfect for a summer barbecue or a quick weeknight dinner. Enjoy!

Tuna Salad Lettuce Wraps

Ingredients:

- 2 cans (5 oz each) of tuna, drained
- 1/4 cup mayonnaise (you can use light mayo or Greek yogurt for a healthier option)
- 1 tablespoon Dijon mustard
- 1/4 cup diced red onion
- 1/4 cup diced celery
- 1/4 cup diced red bell pepper
- 1 tablespoon chopped fresh parsley (optional)
- Salt and pepper to taste
- Lettuce leaves, washed and dried (such as romaine, butter lettuce, or iceberg)

Instructions:

1. In a medium-sized bowl, combine the drained tuna, mayonnaise, Dijon mustard, diced red onion, diced celery, diced red bell pepper, and chopped parsley (if using).
2. Mix all the ingredients together until well combined. Taste and season with salt and pepper according to your preference.
3. Place a spoonful of the tuna salad mixture onto each lettuce leaf.
4. Fold or roll the lettuce leaves around the tuna salad mixture, creating wraps.
5. Serve immediately, or refrigerate until ready to eat.

These tuna salad lettuce wraps are versatile and can be customized to suit your taste. You can add other ingredients like diced cucumber, shredded carrots, avocado slices, or chopped nuts for extra flavor and texture. Enjoy your light and tasty meal!

Roasted Brussels Sprouts with Balsamic Glaze

Ingredients:

- 1 pound Brussels sprouts, trimmed and halved
- 2 tablespoons olive oil
- Salt and pepper to taste
- 2-3 tablespoons balsamic glaze (store-bought or homemade)

For the balsamic glaze:

- 1/2 cup balsamic vinegar
- 1 tablespoon honey or maple syrup (optional for sweetness)

Instructions:

1. Preheat your oven to 400°F (200°C).
2. In a large bowl, toss the halved Brussels sprouts with olive oil until evenly coated. Season with salt and pepper to taste.
3. Arrange the Brussels sprouts in a single layer on a baking sheet lined with parchment paper or aluminum foil, cut side down.
4. Roast the Brussels sprouts in the preheated oven for 20-25 minutes, or until they are tender and caramelized, stirring halfway through the cooking time for even browning.
5. While the Brussels sprouts are roasting, prepare the balsamic glaze. In a small saucepan, bring the balsamic vinegar to a simmer over medium heat. If using honey or maple syrup, add it to the vinegar and stir to combine.
6. Cook the vinegar for about 10-15 minutes, or until it has thickened and reduced by about half, stirring occasionally. It should have a syrupy consistency.
7. Once the Brussels sprouts are done roasting, transfer them to a serving dish and drizzle with the balsamic glaze.
8. Serve the roasted Brussels sprouts with balsamic glaze immediately as a delicious side dish or appetizer.

These roasted Brussels sprouts with balsamic glaze are a wonderful combination of sweet and tangy flavors, with caramelized edges that add depth to the dish. Enjoy!

Turkey and Veggie Meatballs

Ingredients:

- 1 pound ground turkey (you can use lean or extra lean)
- 1 cup grated zucchini, excess moisture squeezed out
- 1/2 cup grated carrot
- 1/4 cup finely chopped onion
- 2 cloves garlic, minced
- 1/4 cup breadcrumbs (you can use whole wheat breadcrumbs or almond meal for a gluten-free option)
- 1/4 cup grated Parmesan cheese
- 1 egg
- 1 tablespoon chopped fresh parsley (optional)
- 1 teaspoon dried oregano
- 1/2 teaspoon salt
- 1/4 teaspoon black pepper
- Olive oil for cooking

Instructions:

1. Preheat your oven to 400°F (200°C). Line a baking sheet with parchment paper or lightly grease it with olive oil.
2. In a large bowl, combine the ground turkey, grated zucchini, grated carrot, chopped onion, minced garlic, breadcrumbs, grated Parmesan cheese, egg, chopped fresh parsley (if using), dried oregano, salt, and black pepper. Mix everything together until well combined.
3. Shape the mixture into meatballs, about 1 to 1.5 inches in diameter, and place them on the prepared baking sheet.
4. Drizzle or brush the meatballs lightly with olive oil to help them brown in the oven.
5. Bake the meatballs in the preheated oven for 20-25 minutes, or until they are cooked through and golden brown on the outside.
6. Once cooked, remove the meatballs from the oven and let them cool slightly before serving.

You can serve these turkey and veggie meatballs with your favorite sauce, such as marinara sauce, pesto, or a creamy yogurt sauce. They are perfect for serving over pasta, zucchini noodles, or with a side of steamed vegetables. Enjoy these tasty and nutritious meatballs!

Chicken and Vegetable Curry

Ingredients:

- 1 tablespoon vegetable oil
- 1 onion, chopped
- 2 cloves garlic, minced
- 1 tablespoon grated ginger
- 1 pound boneless, skinless chicken breasts or thighs, cut into bite-sized pieces
- 2 tablespoons curry powder
- 1 teaspoon ground cumin
- 1 teaspoon ground coriander
- 1/2 teaspoon turmeric powder
- 1/4 teaspoon cayenne pepper (adjust to taste)
- 1 can (14 oz) coconut milk
- 1 cup chicken broth
- 2 cups mixed vegetables (such as bell peppers, carrots, potatoes, peas, etc.), chopped
- Salt and pepper to taste
- Fresh cilantro leaves for garnish (optional)
- Cooked rice or naan bread for serving

Instructions:

1. Heat the vegetable oil in a large skillet or pot over medium heat. Add the chopped onion and cook until softened, about 3-4 minutes.
2. Add the minced garlic and grated ginger to the skillet and cook for an additional 1-2 minutes, until fragrant.
3. Add the chicken pieces to the skillet and cook until they are browned on all sides, about 5-6 minutes.
4. Stir in the curry powder, ground cumin, ground coriander, turmeric powder, and cayenne pepper. Cook for 1-2 minutes, stirring constantly, until the spices are fragrant.
5. Pour in the coconut milk and chicken broth, stirring to combine. Bring the mixture to a simmer.
6. Add the chopped mixed vegetables to the skillet. Cover and simmer for 15-20 minutes, or until the chicken is cooked through and the vegetables are tender.
7. Season the curry with salt and pepper to taste.

8. Serve the chicken and vegetable curry hot, garnished with fresh cilantro leaves if desired. Enjoy with cooked rice or naan bread.

This chicken and vegetable curry is rich, creamy, and full of aromatic spices. It's a hearty and satisfying dish that's sure to please everyone at the table. Enjoy!

Greek Salad with Grilled Chicken

Ingredients:

For the Greek salad:

- 2 large tomatoes, chopped
- 1 cucumber, chopped
- 1 red onion, thinly sliced
- 1 bell pepper (red, yellow, or green), chopped
- 1/2 cup Kalamata olives, pitted
- 1/2 cup crumbled feta cheese
- 2 tablespoons extra virgin olive oil
- 1 tablespoon red wine vinegar
- 1 teaspoon dried oregano
- Salt and pepper to taste
- Optional: 1/4 cup chopped fresh parsley or basil for garnish

For the grilled chicken:

- 2 boneless, skinless chicken breasts
- 2 tablespoons olive oil
- 2 cloves garlic, minced
- 1 teaspoon dried oregano
- Salt and pepper to taste
- Juice of 1 lemon

Instructions:

1. Preheat your grill or grill pan over medium-high heat.
2. In a bowl, whisk together the olive oil, minced garlic, dried oregano, salt, pepper, and lemon juice to make the marinade for the chicken.
3. Place the chicken breasts in a shallow dish or a resealable plastic bag, and pour the marinade over them. Make sure the chicken is well coated. Let it marinate for at least 30 minutes, or up to 4 hours in the refrigerator.

4. While the chicken is marinating, prepare the Greek salad. In a large bowl, combine the chopped tomatoes, cucumber, red onion, bell pepper, Kalamata olives, and crumbled feta cheese.
5. In a small bowl, whisk together the extra virgin olive oil, red wine vinegar, dried oregano, salt, and pepper to make the dressing for the salad.
6. Pour the dressing over the salad ingredients and toss until everything is evenly coated. Taste and adjust the seasoning if needed. Garnish with chopped fresh parsley or basil if desired.
7. Grill the marinated chicken breasts for about 6-8 minutes per side, or until they are cooked through and no longer pink in the center. The cooking time may vary depending on the thickness of the chicken breasts.
8. Once the chicken is done, remove it from the grill and let it rest for a few minutes before slicing it.
9. Serve the grilled chicken slices on top of the Greek salad. You can also serve some crusty bread or pita bread on the side if desired.

This Greek salad with grilled chicken is fresh, flavorful, and perfect for a light and satisfying meal. Enjoy the combination of juicy grilled chicken with the crisp vegetables and tangy feta cheese!

Whole Wheat Pasta Primavera

Ingredients:

- 8 ounces whole wheat pasta (such as spaghetti or penne)
- 2 tablespoons olive oil
- 3 cloves garlic, minced
- 1 small onion, finely chopped
- 1 bell pepper, thinly sliced
- 1 small zucchini, thinly sliced
- 1 small yellow squash, thinly sliced
- 1 cup cherry tomatoes, halved
- 1 cup broccoli florets
- 1/2 cup sliced mushrooms
- Salt and pepper to taste
- 1/4 teaspoon red pepper flakes (optional)
- 1/4 cup grated Parmesan cheese (optional)
- Fresh basil leaves for garnish (optional)

Instructions:

1. Cook the whole wheat pasta according to the package instructions until al dente. Drain and set aside, reserving about 1/2 cup of the pasta cooking water.
2. While the pasta is cooking, heat the olive oil in a large skillet over medium heat. Add the minced garlic and chopped onion, and sauté for 2-3 minutes, or until the onion is softened and translucent.
3. Add the sliced bell pepper, zucchini, yellow squash, cherry tomatoes, broccoli florets, and sliced mushrooms to the skillet. Season with salt, pepper, and red pepper flakes (if using). Cook, stirring occasionally, for 5-7 minutes, or until the vegetables are tender-crisp.
4. Add the cooked whole wheat pasta to the skillet with the vegetables. Toss everything together until the pasta and vegetables are evenly combined.
5. If the pasta seems dry, add some of the reserved pasta cooking water, a little at a time, until you reach your desired consistency.
6. Taste and adjust the seasoning if needed. If desired, sprinkle grated Parmesan cheese over the pasta primavera and garnish with fresh basil leaves before serving.

7. Serve the whole wheat pasta primavera immediately as a nutritious and satisfying meal.

This whole wheat pasta primavera is versatile, so feel free to customize it with your favorite vegetables or add protein like grilled chicken or shrimp if desired. Enjoy this wholesome and flavorful dish!

Quinoa Stuffed Bell Peppers

Ingredients:

- 4 large bell peppers, any color
- 1 cup quinoa, rinsed
- 2 cups vegetable broth or water
- 1 tablespoon olive oil
- 1 small onion, finely chopped
- 2 cloves garlic, minced
- 1 medium carrot, finely chopped
- 1 rib celery, finely chopped
- 1 small zucchini, finely chopped
- 1 cup diced tomatoes (canned or fresh)
- 1 teaspoon dried oregano
- 1 teaspoon dried basil
- 1/2 teaspoon paprika
- Salt and pepper to taste
- 1 cup grated cheese (such as cheddar, mozzarella, or feta), divided
- Fresh parsley or basil for garnish (optional)

Instructions:

1. Preheat your oven to 375°F (190°C). Grease a baking dish large enough to hold the bell peppers.
2. Cut the tops off the bell peppers and remove the seeds and membranes. Set aside.
3. In a medium saucepan, bring the vegetable broth or water to a boil. Add the rinsed quinoa, reduce the heat to low, cover, and simmer for about 15 minutes, or until the quinoa is cooked and the liquid is absorbed. Remove from heat and fluff the quinoa with a fork.
4. While the quinoa is cooking, heat the olive oil in a large skillet over medium heat. Add the chopped onion and cook until softened, about 3-4 minutes. Add the minced garlic and cook for an additional minute, until fragrant.
5. Add the chopped carrot, celery, and zucchini to the skillet. Cook, stirring occasionally, for about 5-7 minutes, or until the vegetables are tender.
6. Stir in the diced tomatoes, dried oregano, dried basil, paprika, salt, and pepper. Cook for another 2-3 minutes to allow the flavors to meld together.

7. Remove the skillet from heat and stir in the cooked quinoa and half of the grated cheese until well combined.
8. Stuff each bell pepper with the quinoa and vegetable mixture, pressing down gently to pack the filling.
9. Place the stuffed bell peppers in the prepared baking dish. Sprinkle the remaining grated cheese over the tops of the stuffed peppers.
10. Cover the baking dish with aluminum foil and bake in the preheated oven for 25-30 minutes, or until the peppers are tender and the cheese is melted and bubbly.
11. Remove the foil and bake for an additional 5-10 minutes, or until the cheese is golden brown.
12. Remove the stuffed bell peppers from the oven and let them cool for a few minutes before serving. Garnish with fresh parsley or basil if desired.

These quinoa stuffed bell peppers are not only delicious but also nutritious and filling.

They make a great vegetarian main course or a hearty side dish. Enjoy!

Roasted Beet and Goat Cheese Salad

Ingredients:

- 3 medium beets, trimmed and scrubbed
- 2 tablespoons olive oil
- Salt and pepper to taste
- 4 cups mixed salad greens (such as arugula, spinach, or spring mix)
- 1/4 cup chopped walnuts or pecans, toasted
- 1/4 cup crumbled goat cheese
- Balsamic glaze or balsamic vinaigrette for dressing

Instructions:

1. Preheat your oven to 400°F (200°C). Line a baking sheet with parchment paper or aluminum foil for easy cleanup.
2. Place the trimmed and scrubbed beets on the prepared baking sheet. Drizzle with olive oil and season with salt and pepper, tossing to coat evenly.
3. Roast the beets in the preheated oven for 40-50 minutes, or until they are tender when pierced with a fork. The roasting time may vary depending on the size of the beets. Once roasted, remove them from the oven and let them cool slightly.
4. While the beets are cooling, toast the chopped walnuts or pecans in a dry skillet over medium heat for 3-4 minutes, or until lightly golden and fragrant. Be sure to watch them carefully to prevent burning. Remove from heat and set aside.
5. Once the beets are cool enough to handle, peel off the skins using your fingers or a small knife. Cut the roasted beets into wedges or slices.
6. Arrange the mixed salad greens on a serving platter or individual salad plates.
7. Top the greens with the roasted beet slices or wedges.
8. Sprinkle the crumbled goat cheese and toasted nuts over the beets.
9. Drizzle the salad with balsamic glaze or balsamic vinaigrette dressing just before serving.
10. Serve the roasted beet and goat cheese salad immediately as a delicious and nutritious appetizer or side dish.

This salad is both visually stunning and delicious, with the sweetness of the roasted beets complementing the tangy goat cheese perfectly. Enjoy!

Eggplant Parmesan with Marinara Sauce

Ingredients:

For the eggplant:

- 2 medium eggplants, sliced into 1/2-inch rounds
- Salt
- 2 cups all-purpose flour (or breadcrumbs for a gluten-free option)
- 4 large eggs, beaten
- 2 cups breadcrumbs (or almond meal for a gluten-free option)
- 1 cup grated Parmesan cheese
- 2 teaspoons dried Italian seasoning (or a mixture of dried basil, oregano, and thyme)
- Olive oil for frying

For the marinara sauce:

- 2 tablespoons olive oil
- 1 onion, finely chopped
- 3 cloves garlic, minced
- 1 can (28 oz) crushed tomatoes
- 1 teaspoon dried oregano
- 1 teaspoon dried basil
- 1/2 teaspoon dried thyme
- Salt and pepper to taste
- Pinch of red pepper flakes (optional)
- Fresh basil leaves for garnish (optional)
- Mozzarella cheese, shredded (optional)

Instructions:

1. Preheat your oven to 375°F (190°C). Grease a baking sheet with olive oil or line it with parchment paper.
2. Place the sliced eggplant rounds on a baking sheet and sprinkle them generously with salt. Let them sit for about 15-20 minutes to allow the excess moisture to be drawn out. Pat the eggplant slices dry with paper towels.

3. Set up a breading station with three shallow bowls. Place the flour (or breadcrumbs) in one bowl, the beaten eggs in another bowl, and the breadcrumbs (or almond meal) mixed with grated Parmesan cheese and dried Italian seasoning in the third bowl.
4. Dredge each eggplant slice in the flour, shaking off any excess. Dip it into the beaten eggs, then coat it evenly with the breadcrumb mixture. Repeat with the remaining eggplant slices.
5. Heat a generous amount of olive oil in a large skillet over medium-high heat. Working in batches, fry the breaded eggplant slices for 2-3 minutes per side, or until golden brown and crispy. Transfer the fried eggplant slices to a plate lined with paper towels to drain excess oil.
6. To make the marinara sauce, heat olive oil in a saucepan over medium heat. Add the chopped onion and cook until softened, about 5 minutes. Add the minced garlic and cook for an additional minute, until fragrant.
7. Stir in the crushed tomatoes, dried oregano, dried basil, dried thyme, salt, pepper, and red pepper flakes (if using). Bring the sauce to a simmer and let it cook for 10-15 minutes, stirring occasionally, until it thickens slightly.
8. Spread a thin layer of marinara sauce on the bottom of a baking dish. Arrange a layer of fried eggplant slices on top of the sauce. Repeat the layers until all the eggplant slices are used, finishing with a layer of marinara sauce on top.
9. If desired, sprinkle shredded mozzarella cheese over the top of the eggplant Parmesan.
10. Bake the eggplant Parmesan in the preheated oven for 25-30 minutes, or until the cheese is melted and bubbly.
11. Remove the baked eggplant Parmesan from the oven and let it cool slightly before serving. Garnish with fresh basil leaves if desired.
12. Serve the eggplant Parmesan hot as a delicious main course, accompanied by a side of pasta or a green salad.

This eggplant Parmesan with marinara sauce is a hearty and satisfying dish that's perfect for a family dinner or special occasion. Enjoy!

Spaghetti Squash with Tomato Basil Sauce

Ingredients:

For the spaghetti squash:

- 1 medium spaghetti squash
- Olive oil
- Salt and pepper to taste

For the tomato basil sauce:

- 2 tablespoons olive oil
- 3 cloves garlic, minced
- 1 can (28 oz) crushed tomatoes
- 1 teaspoon dried oregano
- 1 teaspoon dried basil
- Salt and pepper to taste
- Fresh basil leaves, chopped, for garnish
- Grated Parmesan cheese, for serving (optional)

Instructions:

1. Preheat your oven to 400°F (200°C). Line a baking sheet with parchment paper or aluminum foil.
2. Carefully cut the spaghetti squash in half lengthwise. Scoop out the seeds and stringy pulp from the center using a spoon.
3. Drizzle the cut sides of the spaghetti squash with olive oil and season with salt and pepper. Place the squash halves cut side down on the prepared baking sheet.
4. Roast the spaghetti squash in the preheated oven for 35-45 minutes, or until the flesh is tender and easily pierced with a fork.
5. While the squash is roasting, prepare the tomato basil sauce. Heat olive oil in a saucepan over medium heat. Add the minced garlic and cook for 1-2 minutes, or until fragrant.
6. Stir in the crushed tomatoes, dried oregano, dried basil, salt, and pepper. Bring the sauce to a simmer and let it cook for 10-15 minutes, stirring occasionally, to allow the flavors to meld together.

7. Once the spaghetti squash is cooked, remove it from the oven and let it cool slightly. Use a fork to scrape the flesh of the squash into strands, resembling spaghetti noodles.
8. Divide the spaghetti squash noodles among serving plates or bowls. Top with the tomato basil sauce.
9. Garnish the spaghetti squash with chopped fresh basil leaves and grated Parmesan cheese, if desired.
10. Serve the spaghetti squash with tomato basil sauce hot as a nutritious and satisfying meal.

This spaghetti squash with tomato basil sauce is a light, flavorful, and low-carb alternative to traditional pasta dishes. Enjoy its deliciousness!

Grilled Chicken Caesar Salad

Ingredients:

For the grilled chicken:

- 2 boneless, skinless chicken breasts
- 2 tablespoons olive oil
- 2 cloves garlic, minced
- 1 teaspoon dried oregano
- Salt and pepper to taste
- Juice of 1 lemon

For the Caesar salad:

- 1 large head of romaine lettuce, washed and chopped
- 1/2 cup Caesar dressing (store-bought or homemade)
- 1/2 cup grated Parmesan cheese
- Croutons (store-bought or homemade), for serving

Instructions:

1. Preheat your grill or grill pan over medium-high heat.
2. In a small bowl, whisk together the olive oil, minced garlic, dried oregano, salt, pepper, and lemon juice to make the marinade for the chicken.
3. Place the chicken breasts in a shallow dish or a resealable plastic bag, and pour the marinade over them. Make sure the chicken is well coated. Let it marinate for at least 30 minutes, or up to 4 hours in the refrigerator.
4. Once the chicken has marinated, remove it from the marinade and discard any excess marinade.
5. Grill the chicken breasts for about 6-8 minutes per side, or until they are cooked through and no longer pink in the center. The cooking time may vary depending on the thickness of the chicken breasts. Make sure to flip the chicken halfway through the cooking time for even cooking.
6. Once the chicken is done, remove it from the grill and let it rest for a few minutes before slicing it into strips or cubes.

7. While the chicken is resting, prepare the Caesar salad. In a large salad bowl, toss the chopped romaine lettuce with the Caesar dressing until evenly coated.
8. Add the grated Parmesan cheese to the salad and toss again to combine.
9. Divide the Caesar salad among serving plates or bowls. Top each serving with the sliced or cubed grilled chicken.
10. Garnish the grilled chicken Caesar salad with croutons and additional grated Parmesan cheese if desired.
11. Serve the salad immediately as a delicious and satisfying meal.

This grilled chicken Caesar salad is perfect for a light and flavorful lunch or dinner. Enjoy the combination of smoky grilled chicken with the crisp romaine lettuce and creamy Caesar dressing!

Roasted Asparagus with Lemon and Parmesan

Ingredients:

- 1 pound fresh asparagus spears, woody ends trimmed
- 2 tablespoons olive oil
- Zest of 1 lemon
- Juice of 1/2 lemon
- 1/4 cup grated Parmesan cheese
- Salt and pepper to taste

Instructions:

1. Preheat your oven to 425°F (220°C).
2. Place the trimmed asparagus spears on a baking sheet lined with parchment paper or aluminum foil.
3. Drizzle the olive oil over the asparagus and toss to coat evenly. Season with salt and pepper to taste.
4. Roast the asparagus in the preheated oven for 10-15 minutes, or until they are tender and slightly crispy on the edges. The cooking time may vary depending on the thickness of the asparagus spears, so keep an eye on them to prevent overcooking.
5. While the asparagus is roasting, zest the lemon and squeeze the juice.
6. Once the asparagus is done roasting, remove it from the oven and transfer it to a serving platter.
7. Drizzle the roasted asparagus with the fresh lemon juice and sprinkle the lemon zest over the top.
8. Sprinkle the grated Parmesan cheese evenly over the roasted asparagus.
9. Serve the roasted asparagus with lemon and Parmesan immediately as a delicious and nutritious side dish.

This roasted asparagus with lemon and Parmesan is a perfect accompaniment to any meal. Enjoy its bright flavors and tender texture!

Teriyaki Salmon with Steamed Broccoli

Ingredients:

For the teriyaki salmon:

- 4 salmon fillets, skin-on or skinless
- 1/4 cup soy sauce
- 2 tablespoons honey or maple syrup
- 1 tablespoon rice vinegar
- 1 tablespoon sesame oil
- 2 cloves garlic, minced
- 1 teaspoon grated ginger
- 1 tablespoon cornstarch (optional, for thickening the sauce)
- Sesame seeds and chopped green onions for garnish (optional)

For the steamed broccoli:

- 1 head of broccoli, cut into florets
- Water for steaming
- Salt to taste

Instructions:

1. In a small bowl, whisk together the soy sauce, honey or maple syrup, rice vinegar, sesame oil, minced garlic, and grated ginger to make the teriyaki sauce.
2. If you prefer a thicker sauce, you can mix 1 tablespoon of cornstarch with 2 tablespoons of water to make a slurry. Stir the slurry into the teriyaki sauce mixture.
3. Place the salmon fillets in a shallow dish or a resealable plastic bag. Pour the teriyaki sauce over the salmon, making sure it's evenly coated. Let the salmon marinate for at least 30 minutes in the refrigerator.
4. While the salmon is marinating, prepare the broccoli. Place the broccoli florets in a steamer basket set over a pot of boiling water. Cover and steam for about 5-7 minutes, or until the broccoli is tender but still crisp. Season with salt to taste.
5. Preheat your oven to 400°F (200°C). Line a baking sheet with parchment paper or aluminum foil for easy cleanup.

6. Remove the salmon from the marinade and place it on the prepared baking sheet. Reserve the marinade for later.
7. Bake the salmon in the preheated oven for 12-15 minutes, or until it flakes easily with a fork and is cooked to your desired doneness.
8. While the salmon is baking, transfer the reserved teriyaki marinade to a small saucepan. Bring it to a simmer over medium heat and let it cook for 2-3 minutes, or until it thickens slightly.
9. Once the salmon is done baking, brush it with the thickened teriyaki sauce.
10. Serve the teriyaki salmon with steamed broccoli on the side. Garnish with sesame seeds and chopped green onions if desired.

This teriyaki salmon with steamed broccoli is a flavorful and nutritious meal that's perfect for a weeknight dinner. Enjoy!

Lentil and Vegetable Stir-Fry

Ingredients:

- 1 cup dried lentils, rinsed and drained
- 2 cups water or vegetable broth
- 2 tablespoons olive oil
- 2 cloves garlic, minced
- 1 onion, chopped
- 2 carrots, sliced
- 1 bell pepper, sliced
- 1 zucchini, sliced
- 1 cup broccoli florets
- 1 cup sliced mushrooms
- 1/4 cup soy sauce or tamari
- 1 tablespoon rice vinegar
- 1 tablespoon maple syrup or honey
- 1 teaspoon grated ginger
- 1 tablespoon cornstarch (optional, for thickening the sauce)
- Cooked rice or quinoa for serving
- Sesame seeds and chopped green onions for garnish (optional)

Instructions:

1. In a medium saucepan, combine the dried lentils and water or vegetable broth. Bring to a boil, then reduce the heat to low, cover, and simmer for 20-25 minutes, or until the lentils are tender. Drain any excess liquid and set aside.
2. In a large skillet or wok, heat the olive oil over medium-high heat. Add the minced garlic and chopped onion, and cook for 2-3 minutes, or until softened.
3. Add the sliced carrots, bell pepper, zucchini, broccoli florets, and sliced mushrooms to the skillet. Cook, stirring frequently, for 5-7 minutes, or until the vegetables are tender-crisp.
4. In a small bowl, whisk together the soy sauce or tamari, rice vinegar, maple syrup or honey, and grated ginger to make the sauce.
5. If you prefer a thicker sauce, you can mix 1 tablespoon of cornstarch with 2 tablespoons of water to make a slurry. Stir the slurry into the sauce mixture.

6. Add the cooked lentils to the skillet with the vegetables. Pour the sauce over the lentil and vegetable mixture, stirring to coat everything evenly. Cook for an additional 2-3 minutes, or until the sauce has thickened slightly.
7. Remove the skillet from the heat and serve the lentil and vegetable stir-fry hot over cooked rice or quinoa.
8. Garnish with sesame seeds and chopped green onions if desired.

This lentil and vegetable stir-fry is a delicious and satisfying vegetarian meal that's packed with protein and fiber. Enjoy its flavorful combination of vegetables and savory sauce!

Turkey and Black Bean Chili

Ingredients:

- 1 tablespoon olive oil
- 1 onion, chopped
- 3 cloves garlic, minced
- 1 pound ground turkey
- 2 tablespoons chili powder
- 1 teaspoon ground cumin
- 1/2 teaspoon paprika
- 1/4 teaspoon cayenne pepper (optional, for heat)
- 1 can (14 oz) diced tomatoes
- 1 can (14 oz) black beans, drained and rinsed
- 1 bell pepper, chopped
- 1 cup corn kernels (fresh, frozen, or canned)
- 2 cups chicken broth
- Salt and pepper to taste
- Optional toppings: shredded cheese, chopped green onions, diced avocado, sour cream, cilantro, lime wedges

Instructions:

1. Heat the olive oil in a large pot or Dutch oven over medium heat. Add the chopped onion and minced garlic, and cook for 3-4 minutes, or until softened.
2. Add the ground turkey to the pot, breaking it apart with a spoon, and cook until browned and no longer pink, about 5-6 minutes.
3. Stir in the chili powder, ground cumin, paprika, and cayenne pepper (if using). Cook for 1-2 minutes, stirring constantly, until the spices are fragrant.
4. Add the diced tomatoes (with their juices), black beans, chopped bell pepper, corn kernels, and chicken broth to the pot. Stir to combine.
5. Bring the chili to a simmer, then reduce the heat to low. Cover and let it simmer for 20-25 minutes, stirring occasionally, to allow the flavors to meld together and the chili to thicken.
6. Taste the chili and season with salt and pepper to taste.
7. Serve the turkey and black bean chili hot, garnished with your favorite toppings such as shredded cheese, chopped green onions, diced avocado, sour cream, cilantro, or lime wedges.

8. Enjoy this delicious and comforting chili on its own or with a side of crusty bread or cornbread.

This turkey and black bean chili is a satisfying and nutritious meal that's perfect for chilly days. Enjoy its hearty flavors and warming spices!

Caprese Salad with Fresh Mozzarella

Ingredients:

- 2 large ripe tomatoes, sliced
- 1 ball fresh mozzarella cheese, sliced
- Fresh basil leaves
- Extra virgin olive oil
- Balsamic glaze or balsamic vinegar
- Salt and pepper to taste

Instructions:

1. Start by slicing the tomatoes and fresh mozzarella into rounds of equal thickness, about 1/4 inch thick.
2. Arrange the tomato slices on a serving platter, alternating with slices of fresh mozzarella cheese.
3. Tuck fresh basil leaves between the tomato and mozzarella slices, scattering them evenly across the platter.
4. Drizzle extra virgin olive oil over the tomato and mozzarella slices, ensuring each slice gets a bit of oil.
5. Drizzle balsamic glaze or balsamic vinegar over the salad in a zigzag pattern. You can adjust the amount according to your taste preference.
6. Season the salad with salt and pepper to taste. Remember that the cheese and balsamic glaze can be salty, so go easy on the salt.
7. Optionally, you can garnish the salad with additional fresh basil leaves for extra flavor and presentation.
8. Serve the Caprese salad immediately as a refreshing appetizer or side dish.

This Caprese salad with fresh mozzarella is simple, elegant, and bursting with fresh flavors. Enjoy it as a light and satisfying dish on its own or as part of a larger meal.

Baked Chicken Breast with Herbs

Ingredients:

- 4 boneless, skinless chicken breasts
- 2 tablespoons olive oil
- 2 cloves garlic, minced
- 1 tablespoon fresh lemon juice
- 1 teaspoon dried thyme
- 1 teaspoon dried rosemary
- 1 teaspoon dried oregano
- 1/2 teaspoon dried basil
- Salt and pepper to taste
- Fresh parsley or basil for garnish (optional)
- Lemon wedges for serving (optional)

Instructions:

1. Preheat your oven to 400°F (200°C). Grease a baking dish large enough to hold the chicken breasts in a single layer.
2. In a small bowl, whisk together the olive oil, minced garlic, fresh lemon juice, dried thyme, dried rosemary, dried oregano, dried basil, salt, and pepper to make the herb marinade.
3. Place the chicken breasts in the prepared baking dish. Brush the herb marinade over both sides of the chicken breasts, ensuring they are evenly coated.
4. If you have time, you can let the chicken breasts marinate in the refrigerator for 30 minutes to 1 hour to allow the flavors to penetrate the meat. However, if you're short on time, you can proceed with baking immediately.
5. Once the chicken breasts are marinated, transfer the baking dish to the preheated oven.
6. Bake the chicken breasts for 20-25 minutes, or until they are cooked through and the internal temperature reaches 165°F (75°C). Cooking time may vary depending on the thickness of the chicken breasts, so keep an eye on them to prevent overcooking.
7. Once the chicken breasts are done baking, remove them from the oven and let them rest for a few minutes before serving.
8. Garnish the baked chicken breasts with fresh parsley or basil if desired, and serve them hot with lemon wedges on the side for squeezing over the chicken.

This baked chicken breast with herbs is tender, juicy, and packed with flavor from the aromatic herbs and garlic. Enjoy it as a main dish alongside your favorite sides, such as roasted vegetables or a fresh salad.

Veggie and Bean Burrito Bowl

Ingredients:

For the beans:

- 1 can (15 oz) black beans, drained and rinsed
- 1 tablespoon olive oil
- 2 cloves garlic, minced
- 1 teaspoon ground cumin
- 1 teaspoon chili powder
- Salt and pepper to taste

For the veggies:

- 1 tablespoon olive oil
- 1 onion, diced
- 1 bell pepper, diced
- 1 zucchini, diced
- 1 cup corn kernels (fresh, frozen, or canned)
- 1 teaspoon ground cumin
- 1 teaspoon chili powder
- Salt and pepper to taste

For the bowl:

- Cooked rice (white or brown)
- Sliced avocado
- Salsa
- Chopped fresh cilantro
- Lime wedges for serving

Instructions:

1. Start by preparing the beans. Heat olive oil in a skillet over medium heat. Add minced garlic and cook for 1 minute, until fragrant. Add the black beans, ground

cumin, chili powder, salt, and pepper. Cook for 5-7 minutes, stirring occasionally, until the beans are heated through and the flavors are well combined. Set aside.
2. In the same skillet, heat another tablespoon of olive oil over medium heat. Add diced onion and cook for 2-3 minutes until softened.
3. Add diced bell pepper, diced zucchini, and corn kernels to the skillet. Season with ground cumin, chili powder, salt, and pepper. Cook for 5-7 minutes, stirring occasionally, until the vegetables are tender but still crisp.
4. Assemble the burrito bowls by dividing cooked rice among serving bowls. Top with the cooked beans and sautéed veggies.
5. Add sliced avocado, salsa, and chopped fresh cilantro on top of the beans and veggies.
6. Serve the veggie and bean burrito bowls with lime wedges on the side for squeezing over the bowl before eating.
7. Enjoy your delicious and nutritious veggie and bean burrito bowl!

Feel free to customize your burrito bowl with your favorite toppings such as shredded cheese, sour cream, diced tomatoes, or hot sauce. This meal is versatile, satisfying, and perfect for a quick and easy dinner or lunch option.

Roasted Vegetable and Hummus Wrap

Ingredients:

For the roasted vegetables:

- 1 medium zucchini, sliced
- 1 medium yellow squash, sliced
- 1 bell pepper, sliced
- 1 red onion, sliced
- 2 tablespoons olive oil
- Salt and pepper to taste
- 1 teaspoon dried herbs (such as thyme, rosemary, or Italian seasoning)

For the wrap:

- 4 large whole wheat or spinach tortillas
- 1 cup hummus (store-bought or homemade)
- Fresh spinach leaves
- Optional additions: sliced cucumber, shredded carrots, avocado slices, sprouts, feta cheese, etc.

Instructions:

1. Preheat your oven to 400°F (200°C). Line a baking sheet with parchment paper or aluminum foil for easy cleanup.
2. In a large bowl, toss together the sliced zucchini, yellow squash, bell pepper, and red onion with olive oil, salt, pepper, and dried herbs until evenly coated.
3. Spread the seasoned vegetables in a single layer on the prepared baking sheet. Roast in the preheated oven for 20-25 minutes, or until the vegetables are tender and slightly caramelized, stirring halfway through the cooking time.
4. While the vegetables are roasting, warm the tortillas in a dry skillet over medium heat for 1-2 minutes per side, or until they are softened and pliable.
5. To assemble the wraps, spread a generous layer of hummus onto each tortilla, leaving a border around the edges.
6. Place a handful of fresh spinach leaves on top of the hummus layer.
7. Arrange the roasted vegetables on top of the spinach leaves.

8. Add any optional additions you desire, such as sliced cucumber, shredded carrots, avocado slices, sprouts, or crumbled feta cheese.
9. Roll up the wraps tightly, tucking in the sides as you go, to enclose the filling.
10. Slice the wraps in half diagonally, if desired, and serve immediately.

These roasted vegetable and hummus wraps are not only delicious but also versatile and customizable. Feel free to experiment with different vegetables, spreads, and additions to suit your taste preferences. Enjoy your flavorful and nutritious lunch!

Quinoa and Black Bean Stuffed Peppers

Ingredients:

- 4 large bell peppers, any color
- 1 cup quinoa, rinsed
- 2 cups vegetable broth or water
- 1 tablespoon olive oil
- 1 onion, diced
- 2 cloves garlic, minced
- 1 can (15 oz) black beans, drained and rinsed
- 1 can (14.5 oz) diced tomatoes, drained
- 1 cup corn kernels (fresh, frozen, or canned)
- 1 teaspoon ground cumin
- 1 teaspoon chili powder
- Salt and pepper to taste
- 1 cup shredded cheese (such as cheddar or Mexican blend), divided
- Fresh cilantro or parsley for garnish (optional)
- Sour cream, salsa, or avocado for serving (optional)

Instructions:

1. Preheat your oven to 375°F (190°C). Grease a baking dish large enough to hold the stuffed peppers.
2. Cut the tops off the bell peppers and remove the seeds and membranes. Place the peppers upright in the prepared baking dish.
3. In a medium saucepan, bring the vegetable broth or water to a boil. Add the rinsed quinoa, reduce the heat to low, cover, and simmer for about 15 minutes, or until the quinoa is cooked and the liquid is absorbed. Remove from heat and fluff the quinoa with a fork.
4. While the quinoa is cooking, heat olive oil in a large skillet over medium heat. Add the diced onion and cook until softened, about 3-4 minutes. Add the minced garlic and cook for an additional minute, until fragrant.
5. Stir in the drained black beans, diced tomatoes, corn kernels, ground cumin, chili powder, salt, and pepper. Cook for another 2-3 minutes to allow the flavors to meld together.
6. Remove the skillet from heat and stir in the cooked quinoa and half of the shredded cheese until well combined.

7. Spoon the quinoa and black bean mixture into the prepared bell peppers, pressing down gently to pack the filling.
8. Sprinkle the remaining shredded cheese over the tops of the stuffed peppers.
9. Cover the baking dish with aluminum foil and bake in the preheated oven for 25-30 minutes, or until the peppers are tender and the cheese is melted and bubbly.
10. Remove the foil and bake for an additional 5-10 minutes, or until the cheese is golden brown.
11. Remove the stuffed peppers from the oven and let them cool for a few minutes before serving.
12. Garnish the stuffed peppers with fresh cilantro or parsley, if desired, and serve with sour cream, salsa, or avocado on the side.

These quinoa and black bean stuffed peppers are a delicious and satisfying vegetarian meal that's packed with protein and fiber. Enjoy!

Greek Yogurt Chicken Salad

Ingredients:

- 2 cups cooked chicken breast, shredded or diced
- 1/2 cup Greek yogurt (plain or flavored, such as plain, lemon, or garlic)
- 1/4 cup diced celery
- 1/4 cup diced red onion
- 1/4 cup diced apple
- 1/4 cup halved red grapes (optional)
- 1/4 cup chopped walnuts or pecans (optional)
- 1 tablespoon lemon juice
- 1 tablespoon Dijon mustard (optional)
- Salt and pepper to taste
- Fresh parsley or dill for garnish (optional)

Instructions:

1. In a large mixing bowl, combine the cooked chicken breast, Greek yogurt, diced celery, diced red onion, diced apple, halved red grapes (if using), and chopped nuts (if using).
2. Add lemon juice and Dijon mustard (if using) to the bowl. Stir well to combine all the ingredients.
3. Season the chicken salad with salt and pepper to taste. Adjust the seasoning according to your preference.
4. If you prefer a creamier consistency, you can add more Greek yogurt. If you prefer a tangier flavor, you can add more lemon juice.
5. Once the chicken salad is well mixed and seasoned to your liking, cover the bowl and refrigerate for at least 30 minutes to allow the flavors to meld together.
6. Before serving, give the chicken salad a final stir and taste test. Adjust the seasoning if necessary.
7. Serve the Greek yogurt chicken salad chilled, garnished with fresh parsley or dill if desired.
8. Enjoy the creamy and flavorful chicken salad on its own, or serve it on bread, wraps, crackers, or a bed of greens for a delicious meal.

This Greek yogurt chicken salad is light, refreshing, and packed with protein. It's perfect for a quick and easy lunch or snack, and you can customize it with your favorite ingredients and seasonings. Enjoy!

Veggie Omelette with Spinach and Mushrooms

Ingredients:

- 2 large eggs
- 1 tablespoon milk or water
- Salt and pepper to taste
- 1 tablespoon olive oil or butter
- 1 cup fresh spinach leaves, roughly chopped
- 1/2 cup sliced mushrooms
- 1/4 cup diced onion
- 1/4 cup diced bell pepper (optional)
- 1/4 cup shredded cheese (such as cheddar, mozzarella, or feta) (optional)
- Fresh herbs for garnish (such as parsley, chives, or basil) (optional)

Instructions:

1. In a small bowl, beat the eggs with the milk or water until well combined. Season with salt and pepper to taste.
2. Heat the olive oil or butter in a non-stick skillet over medium heat.
3. Add the diced onion and sliced mushrooms to the skillet. Cook for 3-4 minutes, stirring occasionally, until the vegetables are softened and lightly browned.
4. Add the chopped spinach leaves to the skillet and cook for an additional 1-2 minutes, or until wilted.
5. Pour the beaten eggs evenly over the cooked vegetables in the skillet. Use a spatula to gently lift the edges of the omelette and tilt the skillet to allow the uncooked eggs to flow to the bottom.
6. Continue cooking the omelette for 2-3 minutes, or until the bottom is set and the top is still slightly runny.
7. If using cheese, sprinkle the shredded cheese evenly over one half of the omelette.
8. Carefully fold the other half of the omelette over the cheese to form a half-moon shape. Press down gently with the spatula to seal.
9. Cook the omelette for another 1-2 minutes, or until the cheese is melted and the omelette is cooked through.
10. Slide the omelette onto a plate and garnish with fresh herbs if desired.
11. Serve the veggie omelette hot as a delicious and nutritious breakfast or brunch option.

Feel free to customize your veggie omelette with your favorite vegetables, cheese, and herbs. You can also serve it with toast, fruit, or a side salad for a complete meal. Enjoy!

Turkey and Quinoa Stuffed Bell Peppers

Ingredients:

- 4 large bell peppers, any color
- 1 cup quinoa, rinsed
- 2 cups vegetable broth or water
- 1 tablespoon olive oil
- 1 onion, diced
- 2 cloves garlic, minced
- 1 pound ground turkey
- 1 can (14.5 oz) diced tomatoes, drained
- 1 cup corn kernels (fresh, frozen, or canned)
- 1 teaspoon ground cumin
- 1 teaspoon chili powder
- Salt and pepper to taste
- 1/2 cup shredded cheese (such as cheddar or Mexican blend)
- Fresh cilantro or parsley for garnish (optional)
- Sour cream or avocado slices for serving (optional)

Instructions:

1. Preheat your oven to 375°F (190°C). Grease a baking dish large enough to hold the stuffed peppers.
2. Cut the tops off the bell peppers and remove the seeds and membranes. Place the peppers upright in the prepared baking dish.
3. In a medium saucepan, bring the vegetable broth or water to a boil. Add the rinsed quinoa, reduce the heat to low, cover, and simmer for about 15 minutes, or until the quinoa is cooked and the liquid is absorbed. Remove from heat and fluff the quinoa with a fork.
4. While the quinoa is cooking, heat olive oil in a large skillet over medium heat. Add the diced onion and cook until softened, about 3-4 minutes. Add the minced garlic and cook for an additional minute, until fragrant.
5. Add the ground turkey to the skillet and cook until browned, breaking it apart with a spoon as it cooks.
6. Stir in the diced tomatoes, corn kernels, ground cumin, chili powder, salt, and pepper. Cook for another 2-3 minutes to allow the flavors to meld together.
7. Remove the skillet from heat and stir in the cooked quinoa until well combined.

8. Spoon the turkey and quinoa mixture into the prepared bell peppers, pressing down gently to pack the filling.
9. Sprinkle the shredded cheese evenly over the tops of the stuffed peppers.
10. Cover the baking dish with aluminum foil and bake in the preheated oven for 25-30 minutes, or until the peppers are tender and the cheese is melted and bubbly.
11. Remove the foil and bake for an additional 5-10 minutes, or until the cheese is golden brown.
12. Remove the stuffed peppers from the oven and let them cool for a few minutes before serving.
13. Garnish the stuffed peppers with fresh cilantro or parsley, if desired, and serve with sour cream or avocado slices on the side.

These turkey and quinoa stuffed bell peppers are a delicious and satisfying meal that's packed with protein and fiber. Enjoy!

Baked Cod with Lemon and Garlic

Ingredients:

- 4 cod fillets (about 6 ounces each)
- 2 tablespoons olive oil
- 4 cloves garlic, minced
- Zest of 1 lemon
- Juice of 1 lemon
- Salt and pepper to taste
- Fresh parsley for garnish (optional)

Instructions:

1. Preheat your oven to 400°F (200°C). Grease a baking dish large enough to hold the cod fillets in a single layer.
2. Pat the cod fillets dry with paper towels and place them in the prepared baking dish.
3. In a small bowl, whisk together the olive oil, minced garlic, lemon zest, lemon juice, salt, and pepper.
4. Pour the lemon-garlic mixture over the cod fillets, making sure they are evenly coated.
5. Bake the cod fillets in the preheated oven for 12-15 minutes, or until they are opaque and flake easily with a fork. Cooking time may vary depending on the thickness of the fillets.
6. Once the cod fillets are done baking, remove them from the oven and let them rest for a few minutes.
7. Garnish the baked cod with fresh parsley, if desired, and serve hot.

This baked cod with lemon and garlic is light, healthy, and bursting with flavor. It's perfect for a quick and easy weeknight dinner. Enjoy!

Cauliflower Fried Rice with Shrimp

Ingredients:

- 1 medium head of cauliflower
- 1 tablespoon sesame oil
- 1 tablespoon olive oil or vegetable oil
- 1 pound shrimp, peeled and deveined
- 2 cloves garlic, minced
- 1 small onion, finely chopped
- 1 cup mixed vegetables (such as diced carrots, peas, and bell peppers)
- 2 eggs, lightly beaten
- 3 tablespoons soy sauce or tamari
- 1 tablespoon rice vinegar
- Salt and pepper to taste
- Green onions, chopped, for garnish (optional)
- Sesame seeds, for garnish (optional)

Instructions:

1. Cut the cauliflower into florets and place them in a food processor. Pulse until the cauliflower resembles rice-like grains. You may need to do this in batches, depending on the size of your food processor.
2. Heat the sesame oil and olive oil or vegetable oil in a large skillet or wok over medium-high heat.
3. Add the shrimp to the skillet and cook for 2-3 minutes on each side, or until they are pink and cooked through. Remove the shrimp from the skillet and set aside.
4. In the same skillet, add the minced garlic and chopped onion. Cook for 2-3 minutes, or until the onion is translucent.
5. Add the mixed vegetables to the skillet and cook for an additional 3-4 minutes, or until they are tender.
6. Push the vegetables to one side of the skillet and add the beaten eggs to the empty side. Scramble the eggs until they are cooked through.
7. Add the riced cauliflower to the skillet and stir to combine with the vegetables and eggs.
8. Return the cooked shrimp to the skillet and stir to combine.
9. In a small bowl, whisk together the soy sauce or tamari and rice vinegar. Pour the sauce over the cauliflower mixture and stir to combine.

10. Cook for an additional 2-3 minutes, stirring occasionally, until everything is heated through and well combined.
11. Season with salt and pepper to taste.
12. Garnish the cauliflower fried rice with chopped green onions and sesame seeds, if desired.
13. Serve hot and enjoy your delicious and nutritious cauliflower fried rice with shrimp!

This dish is low in carbs, high in protein, and packed with flavor. It's a perfect option for a quick and healthy weeknight meal.

Chickpea and Vegetable Tagine

Ingredients:

- 2 tablespoons olive oil
- 1 onion, diced
- 2 cloves garlic, minced
- 1 teaspoon ground cumin
- 1 teaspoon ground coriander
- 1/2 teaspoon ground cinnamon
- 1/2 teaspoon ground ginger
- 1/4 teaspoon ground turmeric
- 1/4 teaspoon cayenne pepper (optional, for heat)
- 1 can (15 oz) chickpeas, drained and rinsed
- 1 can (14.5 oz) diced tomatoes
- 2 carrots, peeled and diced
- 1 zucchini, diced
- 1 cup vegetable broth
- 1/4 cup chopped dried apricots (optional, for sweetness)
- Salt and pepper to taste
- Fresh cilantro or parsley for garnish
- Cooked couscous or rice for serving

Instructions:

1. Heat the olive oil in a large pot or Dutch oven over medium heat. Add the diced onion and cook for 3-4 minutes, or until softened.
2. Add the minced garlic, ground cumin, ground coriander, ground cinnamon, ground ginger, ground turmeric, and cayenne pepper (if using). Cook for 1-2 minutes, stirring constantly, until fragrant.
3. Add the drained and rinsed chickpeas, diced tomatoes, diced carrots, diced zucchini, vegetable broth, and chopped dried apricots (if using) to the pot. Stir to combine.
4. Bring the mixture to a simmer, then reduce the heat to low. Cover and let the tagine simmer for 20-25 minutes, stirring occasionally, or until the vegetables are tender and the flavors have melded together.
5. Taste the tagine and season with salt and pepper to taste.

6. Serve the chickpea and vegetable tagine hot, garnished with fresh cilantro or parsley. Serve with cooked couscous or rice on the side.

This chickpea and vegetable tagine is a satisfying and nutritious meal that's packed with flavor. It's perfect for a cozy dinner on a cold evening. Enjoy!

Spinach and Feta Stuffed Chicken Breast

Ingredients:

- 4 boneless, skinless chicken breasts
- Salt and pepper to taste
- 1 tablespoon olive oil
- 2 cups fresh spinach leaves, chopped
- 1/2 cup crumbled feta cheese
- 2 cloves garlic, minced
- 1 tablespoon chopped fresh parsley (optional)
- 1 tablespoon chopped fresh basil (optional)
- Toothpicks or kitchen twine (optional, for securing the stuffed chicken breasts)

Instructions:

1. Preheat your oven to 375°F (190°C). Grease a baking dish large enough to hold the chicken breasts in a single layer.
2. Use a sharp knife to make a horizontal slit along the side of each chicken breast, creating a pocket for the stuffing. Be careful not to cut all the way through.
3. Season the chicken breasts with salt and pepper to taste, both inside and out.
4. In a skillet, heat the olive oil over medium heat. Add the chopped spinach and minced garlic, and cook for 2-3 minutes, or until the spinach is wilted and the garlic is fragrant.
5. Remove the skillet from the heat and stir in the crumbled feta cheese, chopped fresh parsley, and chopped fresh basil (if using). Mix until the ingredients are well combined.
6. Stuff each chicken breast with the spinach and feta mixture, dividing it evenly among them. Press the edges of the chicken breasts together to seal in the filling. If needed, you can secure the edges with toothpicks or kitchen twine.
7. Place the stuffed chicken breasts in the prepared baking dish.
8. Bake in the preheated oven for 25-30 minutes, or until the chicken is cooked through and no longer pink in the center, with an internal temperature of 165°F (75°C).
9. Once cooked, remove the stuffed chicken breasts from the oven and let them rest for a few minutes before serving.
10. Serve the spinach and feta stuffed chicken breasts hot, garnished with additional fresh herbs if desired.

11. Enjoy your delicious and flavorful stuffed chicken breasts as a main course for a special dinner!

This spinach and feta stuffed chicken breast recipe is sure to impress with its vibrant flavors and elegant presentation. It's a dish that's both delicious and satisfying.

Turkey and Sweet Potato Hash

Ingredients:

- 1 tablespoon olive oil
- 1 pound ground turkey
- 2 medium sweet potatoes, peeled and diced into small cubes
- 1 onion, diced
- 2 cloves garlic, minced
- 1 teaspoon smoked paprika
- 1/2 teaspoon ground cumin
- 1/2 teaspoon dried thyme
- Salt and pepper to taste
- 1 bell pepper, diced
- 1 cup baby spinach leaves
- 4 eggs (optional)
- Fresh parsley or green onions for garnish (optional)

Instructions:

1. Heat the olive oil in a large skillet or cast-iron pan over medium-high heat.
2. Add the ground turkey to the skillet and cook, breaking it apart with a spoon, until it is browned and cooked through, about 5-7 minutes. Remove the cooked turkey from the skillet and set aside.
3. In the same skillet, add the diced sweet potatoes and onion. Cook, stirring occasionally, until the sweet potatoes are tender and lightly browned, about 10-12 minutes.
4. Add the minced garlic, smoked paprika, ground cumin, dried thyme, salt, and pepper to the skillet. Stir to coat the sweet potatoes and onion with the spices.
5. Add the diced bell pepper to the skillet and cook for an additional 2-3 minutes, until it is softened.
6. Return the cooked turkey to the skillet and stir to combine with the sweet potato mixture.
7. Add the baby spinach leaves to the skillet and cook for 1-2 minutes, or until they are wilted.
8. If desired, create four wells in the hash mixture and crack an egg into each well. Cover the skillet and cook for 5-7 minutes, or until the eggs are cooked to your liking.

9. Garnish the turkey and sweet potato hash with fresh parsley or green onions, if desired.
10. Serve hot and enjoy your delicious and satisfying turkey and sweet potato hash!

This dish is versatile and can be customized with your favorite toppings or additional vegetables. It's a nutritious and filling meal that's sure to become a family favorite.

Grilled Vegetable and Hummus Sandwich

Ingredients:

- 1 medium zucchini, sliced lengthwise into strips
- 1 medium yellow squash, sliced lengthwise into strips
- 1 red bell pepper, sliced into strips
- 1 yellow bell pepper, sliced into strips
- 1 small red onion, sliced into rounds
- 2 tablespoons olive oil
- Salt and pepper to taste
- 4 slices of your favorite bread (such as whole wheat, sourdough, or ciabatta)
- 1/2 cup hummus (store-bought or homemade)
- Fresh spinach or lettuce leaves
- Optional additions: sliced tomato, cucumber, avocado, sprouts, etc.

Instructions:

1. Preheat your grill or grill pan to medium-high heat.
2. In a large bowl, toss the sliced zucchini, yellow squash, bell peppers, and red onion with olive oil, salt, and pepper until evenly coated.
3. Grill the vegetables for 3-4 minutes per side, or until they are tender and lightly charred. Remove them from the grill and set aside.
4. While the vegetables are grilling, toast the slices of bread until they are golden brown.
5. To assemble the sandwiches, spread a generous layer of hummus on each slice of toasted bread.
6. Layer the grilled vegetables on top of the hummus, followed by fresh spinach or lettuce leaves and any additional toppings you like.
7. Place another slice of toasted bread on top to complete the sandwiches.
8. If desired, you can slice the sandwiches in half diagonally before serving.
9. Serve the grilled vegetable and hummus sandwiches immediately, and enjoy!

These sandwiches are versatile, so feel free to customize them with your favorite grilled vegetables and additional toppings. They're perfect for a quick and easy lunch or dinner option that's both delicious and nutritious.

Quinoa and Kale Salad with Lemon Dressing

Ingredients:

For the salad:

- 1 cup quinoa, rinsed
- 2 cups water or vegetable broth
- 1 bunch kale, stems removed and leaves chopped
- 1 tablespoon olive oil
- Salt and pepper to taste
- 1/2 cup cherry tomatoes, halved
- 1/2 cup cucumber, diced
- 1/4 cup red onion, thinly sliced
- 1/4 cup toasted nuts or seeds (such as almonds, walnuts, or pumpkin seeds)
- Optional additions: diced bell pepper, shredded carrots, cooked chickpeas, etc.

For the lemon dressing:

- 1/4 cup olive oil
- Zest and juice of 1 lemon
- 1 clove garlic, minced
- 1 teaspoon Dijon mustard
- 1 teaspoon honey or maple syrup (optional, for sweetness)
- Salt and pepper to taste

Instructions:

1. In a medium saucepan, bring the water or vegetable broth to a boil. Add the rinsed quinoa, reduce the heat to low, cover, and simmer for about 15 minutes, or until the quinoa is cooked and the liquid is absorbed. Remove from heat and let it cool slightly.
2. While the quinoa is cooking, massage the chopped kale leaves with 1 tablespoon of olive oil and a pinch of salt for a few minutes until the leaves are tenderized and slightly wilted.

3. In a large salad bowl, combine the cooked quinoa, massaged kale, halved cherry tomatoes, diced cucumber, thinly sliced red onion, and toasted nuts or seeds. Add any optional additions you like.
4. In a small bowl, whisk together the olive oil, lemon zest, lemon juice, minced garlic, Dijon mustard, honey or maple syrup (if using), salt, and pepper to make the lemon dressing.
5. Pour the lemon dressing over the quinoa and kale salad and toss until everything is evenly coated.
6. Taste and adjust the seasoning if necessary.
7. Serve the quinoa and kale salad immediately, or refrigerate it for at least 30 minutes to allow the flavors to meld together before serving.
8. Enjoy your refreshing and nutritious quinoa and kale salad with lemon dressing as a delicious side dish or a light and healthy meal!

This salad is versatile, so feel free to customize it with your favorite vegetables, herbs, or protein sources. It's perfect for meal prep and can be enjoyed as a quick and easy lunch or dinner option.

Broccoli and Cheese Stuffed Chicken Breast

Ingredients:

- 4 boneless, skinless chicken breasts
- Salt and pepper to taste
- 1 cup broccoli florets, steamed until tender and chopped
- 1 cup shredded cheddar cheese (or your favorite cheese)
- 1/4 cup grated Parmesan cheese
- 2 cloves garlic, minced
- 1/2 teaspoon dried thyme
- 1/2 teaspoon dried oregano
- 1/4 teaspoon red pepper flakes (optional, for heat)
- 1 tablespoon olive oil
- Toothpicks or kitchen twine (optional, for securing the stuffed chicken breasts)

Instructions:

1. Preheat your oven to 375°F (190°C). Grease a baking dish large enough to hold the chicken breasts in a single layer.
2. Use a sharp knife to make a horizontal slit along the side of each chicken breast, creating a pocket for the stuffing. Be careful not to cut all the way through.
3. Season the chicken breasts with salt and pepper to taste, both inside and out.
4. In a mixing bowl, combine the chopped broccoli, shredded cheddar cheese, grated Parmesan cheese, minced garlic, dried thyme, dried oregano, and red pepper flakes (if using). Mix well to combine.
5. Stuff each chicken breast with the broccoli and cheese mixture, dividing it evenly among them. Press the edges of the chicken breasts together to seal in the filling. If needed, you can secure the edges with toothpicks or kitchen twine.
6. Heat the olive oil in a large skillet over medium-high heat. Sear the stuffed chicken breasts for 2-3 minutes on each side, or until they are golden brown.
7. Transfer the seared chicken breasts to the prepared baking dish.
8. Bake in the preheated oven for 20-25 minutes, or until the chicken is cooked through and no longer pink in the center, with an internal temperature of 165°F (75°C).
9. Once cooked, remove the stuffed chicken breasts from the oven and let them rest for a few minutes before serving.
10. Serve the broccoli and cheese stuffed chicken breasts hot, and enjoy!

This dish is rich, flavorful, and sure to impress with its gooey cheese and tender chicken. It's perfect for a cozy dinner with loved ones.

Greek Yogurt Pancakes with Fresh Berries

Ingredients:

- 1 cup all-purpose flour (or whole wheat flour for a healthier option)
- 1 tablespoon sugar (optional)
- 1 teaspoon baking powder
- 1/2 teaspoon baking soda
- 1/4 teaspoon salt
- 1 cup Greek yogurt
- 1/2 cup milk (any type you prefer)
- 1 large egg
- 1 teaspoon vanilla extract
- Butter or oil for cooking
- Fresh berries (such as strawberries, blueberries, raspberries) for serving
- Maple syrup or honey for serving

Instructions:

1. In a large mixing bowl, whisk together the flour, sugar (if using), baking powder, baking soda, and salt until well combined.
2. In a separate bowl, mix together the Greek yogurt, milk, egg, and vanilla extract until smooth and well combined.
3. Pour the wet ingredients into the dry ingredients and stir until just combined. Be careful not to overmix; a few lumps in the batter are okay.
4. Heat a non-stick skillet or griddle over medium heat. Add a small amount of butter or oil to the skillet to prevent sticking.
5. Pour about 1/4 cup of batter onto the skillet for each pancake. Cook until bubbles form on the surface of the pancake and the edges begin to look set, about 2-3 minutes.
6. Flip the pancakes and cook for an additional 1-2 minutes on the other side, until golden brown and cooked through.
7. Repeat with the remaining batter, adding more butter or oil to the skillet as needed.
8. Serve the Greek yogurt pancakes hot, topped with fresh berries and drizzled with maple syrup or honey.
9. Enjoy your delicious and nutritious pancakes for a delightful breakfast or brunch!

These Greek yogurt pancakes are fluffy, flavorful, and packed with protein from the yogurt. They're a fantastic way to start your day on a healthy and delicious note!

Baked Chicken and Vegetable Casserole

Ingredients:

- 4 boneless, skinless chicken breasts
- Salt and pepper to taste
- 2 tablespoons olive oil
- 1 onion, diced
- 2 cloves garlic, minced
- 2 carrots, peeled and diced
- 2 stalks celery, diced
- 1 bell pepper, diced
- 1 cup broccoli florets
- 1 cup cauliflower florets
- 1 cup sliced mushrooms
- 1 can (14.5 oz) diced tomatoes, drained
- 1 cup chicken broth
- 1 teaspoon dried thyme
- 1 teaspoon dried rosemary
- 1/2 teaspoon paprika
- 1/4 teaspoon red pepper flakes (optional, for heat)
- 1 cup shredded cheese (such as cheddar or mozzarella)
- Fresh parsley for garnish (optional)

Instructions:

1. Preheat your oven to 375°F (190°C). Grease a baking dish large enough to hold the chicken and vegetables.
2. Season the chicken breasts with salt and pepper to taste. Place them in the prepared baking dish.
3. In a large skillet, heat the olive oil over medium heat. Add the diced onion and minced garlic, and cook for 2-3 minutes, until softened and fragrant.
4. Add the diced carrots, celery, bell pepper, broccoli, cauliflower, and mushrooms to the skillet. Cook for 5-6 minutes, stirring occasionally, until the vegetables are slightly softened.
5. Stir in the diced tomatoes, chicken broth, dried thyme, dried rosemary, paprika, and red pepper flakes (if using). Bring the mixture to a simmer and cook for another 2-3 minutes.

6. Pour the vegetable mixture over the chicken breasts in the baking dish, spreading it out evenly.
7. Cover the baking dish with aluminum foil and bake in the preheated oven for 25-30 minutes, or until the chicken is cooked through.
8. Remove the foil from the baking dish and sprinkle the shredded cheese evenly over the top of the casserole.
9. Return the casserole to the oven and bake for an additional 5-10 minutes, or until the cheese is melted and bubbly.
10. Remove the casserole from the oven and let it cool for a few minutes before serving.
11. Garnish the baked chicken and vegetable casserole with fresh parsley, if desired.
12. Serve hot and enjoy your delicious and wholesome meal!

This baked chicken and vegetable casserole is a complete meal in one dish, packed with protein and a variety of colorful veggies. It's perfect for a family dinner or meal prep for the week ahead.

Lentil and Vegetable Soup

Ingredients:

- 1 tablespoon olive oil
- 1 onion, diced
- 2 cloves garlic, minced
- 2 carrots, diced
- 2 stalks celery, diced
- 1 bell pepper, diced
- 1 cup dried green or brown lentils, rinsed and drained
- 1 can (14.5 oz) diced tomatoes
- 4 cups vegetable broth
- 2 cups water
- 1 teaspoon dried thyme
- 1 teaspoon dried oregano
- 1 bay leaf
- Salt and pepper to taste
- 2 cups chopped spinach or kale
- Juice of 1 lemon (optional)
- Fresh parsley or cilantro for garnish (optional)

Instructions:

1. In a large pot or Dutch oven, heat the olive oil over medium heat. Add the diced onion and cook for 2-3 minutes, until softened.
2. Add the minced garlic, diced carrots, diced celery, and diced bell pepper to the pot. Cook for another 5 minutes, stirring occasionally, until the vegetables are softened.
3. Add the rinsed lentils, diced tomatoes (with their juices), vegetable broth, water, dried thyme, dried oregano, and bay leaf to the pot. Stir to combine.
4. Bring the soup to a simmer, then reduce the heat to low. Cover and let the soup cook for about 20-25 minutes, or until the lentils are tender.
5. Once the lentils are cooked, season the soup with salt and pepper to taste. Adjust the seasoning as needed.
6. Stir in the chopped spinach or kale and let the soup simmer for another 5 minutes, until the greens are wilted.
7. If desired, stir in the lemon juice for a bright and tangy flavor.
8. Remove the bay leaf from the soup and discard.

9. Ladle the lentil and vegetable soup into bowls and garnish with fresh parsley or cilantro, if desired.
10. Serve hot and enjoy your delicious and nutritious soup!

This lentil and vegetable soup is packed with protein, fiber, and vitamins, making it a wholesome and satisfying meal. It's perfect for a cozy dinner or meal prep for a quick and easy lunch throughout the week.

Shrimp and Avocado Salad

Ingredients:

- 1 pound large shrimp, peeled and deveined
- Salt and pepper to taste
- 1 tablespoon olive oil
- 1 teaspoon paprika
- 1/2 teaspoon garlic powder
- 1/2 teaspoon onion powder
- 4 cups mixed salad greens (such as spinach, arugula, or spring mix)
- 1 avocado, diced
- 1 cup cherry tomatoes, halved
- 1/4 cup red onion, thinly sliced
- 1/4 cup fresh cilantro or parsley, chopped
- Juice of 1 lime
- 2 tablespoons extra virgin olive oil
- Salt and pepper to taste

Instructions:

1. Season the shrimp with salt, pepper, paprika, garlic powder, and onion powder. Toss to coat evenly.
2. Heat the olive oil in a large skillet over medium-high heat. Add the seasoned shrimp to the skillet and cook for 2-3 minutes per side, or until they are pink and opaque. Remove from heat and set aside.
3. In a large salad bowl, combine the mixed salad greens, diced avocado, halved cherry tomatoes, thinly sliced red onion, and chopped cilantro or parsley.
4. In a small bowl, whisk together the lime juice, extra virgin olive oil, salt, and pepper to make the dressing.
5. Pour the dressing over the salad ingredients in the bowl and toss to coat evenly.
6. Divide the salad mixture evenly among serving plates or bowls.
7. Top each plate of salad with the cooked shrimp.
8. Serve the shrimp and avocado salad immediately, and enjoy!

This salad is light, refreshing, and packed with protein and healthy fats from the shrimp and avocado. It's perfect for a quick and easy lunch or dinner option that's both delicious and nutritious.

Baked Cod with Herbed Quinoa

Ingredients:

For the baked cod:

- 4 cod fillets (about 6 ounces each)
- Salt and pepper to taste
- 2 tablespoons olive oil
- 2 cloves garlic, minced
- 1 tablespoon chopped fresh parsley
- 1 tablespoon chopped fresh dill (or 1 teaspoon dried dill)
- 1 tablespoon lemon juice
- Lemon wedges for serving

For the herbed quinoa:

- 1 cup quinoa, rinsed
- 2 cups vegetable broth or water
- 1 tablespoon olive oil
- 2 cloves garlic, minced
- 1 teaspoon chopped fresh parsley
- 1 teaspoon chopped fresh dill (or 1/2 teaspoon dried dill)
- Salt and pepper to taste

Instructions:

1. Preheat your oven to 375°F (190°C). Grease a baking dish large enough to hold the cod fillets in a single layer.
2. Season the cod fillets with salt and pepper to taste, and place them in the prepared baking dish.
3. In a small bowl, whisk together the olive oil, minced garlic, chopped parsley, chopped dill, and lemon juice. Pour this mixture over the cod fillets, making sure they are evenly coated.
4. Bake the cod fillets in the preheated oven for 12-15 minutes, or until they are opaque and flake easily with a fork.
5. While the cod is baking, prepare the herbed quinoa. In a medium saucepan, bring the vegetable broth or water to a boil. Add the rinsed quinoa, reduce the heat to

low, cover, and simmer for about 15 minutes, or until the quinoa is cooked and the liquid is absorbed.
6. In a skillet, heat 1 tablespoon of olive oil over medium heat. Add the minced garlic and cook for 1-2 minutes, until fragrant.
7. Add the cooked quinoa to the skillet, along with the chopped parsley, chopped dill, salt, and pepper. Stir to combine and cook for an additional 2-3 minutes to allow the flavors to meld together.
8. Serve the baked cod fillets hot, garnished with lemon wedges, alongside the herbed quinoa.
9. Enjoy your delicious and nutritious baked cod with herbed quinoa!

This dish is light, flavorful, and packed with protein and fiber. It's perfect for a healthy and satisfying meal that's quick and easy to prepare.

Chicken and Vegetable Skillet

Ingredients:

- 1 tablespoon olive oil
- 4 boneless, skinless chicken breasts, cut into bite-sized pieces
- Salt and pepper to taste
- 1 onion, diced
- 2 cloves garlic, minced
- 2 carrots, sliced
- 1 bell pepper, diced
- 1 zucchini, diced
- 1 cup cherry tomatoes, halved
- 1 teaspoon dried oregano
- 1 teaspoon dried basil
- 1/2 teaspoon paprika
- 1/4 teaspoon red pepper flakes (optional, for heat)
- 1/2 cup chicken broth or water
- Fresh parsley or basil for garnish (optional)

Instructions:

1. Heat the olive oil in a large skillet over medium-high heat.
2. Season the chicken pieces with salt and pepper to taste. Add them to the skillet and cook for 5-6 minutes, or until browned and cooked through. Remove the chicken from the skillet and set aside.
3. In the same skillet, add the diced onion and minced garlic. Cook for 2-3 minutes, or until softened and fragrant.
4. Add the sliced carrots, diced bell pepper, and diced zucchini to the skillet. Cook for 5-6 minutes, or until the vegetables are tender-crisp.
5. Stir in the cherry tomatoes, dried oregano, dried basil, paprika, and red pepper flakes (if using). Cook for an additional 2-3 minutes.
6. Return the cooked chicken to the skillet and stir to combine with the vegetables.
7. Pour the chicken broth or water into the skillet, stirring to scrape up any browned bits from the bottom of the pan. Cook for 2-3 minutes, or until the liquid has reduced slightly.
8. Taste and adjust the seasoning with salt and pepper, if needed.
9. Garnish the chicken and vegetable skillet with fresh parsley or basil, if desired.

10. Serve hot and enjoy your delicious and nutritious meal!

This chicken and vegetable skillet is versatile, so feel free to customize it with your favorite vegetables or herbs. It's a satisfying and wholesome dish that's perfect for a quick and easy dinner.